The Joyful Techno-tard

A pretty cool book
for all us low-tech
people living in this
high-tech world

Justin Case

Published by:
Apricot Press
Box 98
Nephi, Utah
84648

books@apricotpress.com
www.apricotpress.com

ISBN 1-885027-48-6

Illustrated & Designed by David Mecham
Printed in the United States of America

Forward

In the Roman Empire, around the year 5 AD, times were changing. The Pax Romana had created security, freedoms, and opportunities previously unheard of. A group of inventors exhibited a new invention for Caesar Augustus-a crude steam engine with multiple applications (apps).

After a season of considering the benefits of the steam engine, Caesar concluded to have it destroyed. His reasoning: It would put thousands of unskilled and uneducated people out of work.

So, it would be sixteen hundred years before the world would have its' steam engine.

In a slightly different way and considering computers instead of steam engines this book takes a new and hopefully light-hearted look at Caesar's dilemma.

Contents

When You are Determined to Remain
Computer Illiterate Even if it Means
You Will be Persecuted, Shunned,
and Isolated.   1

How to Know if You are a Technotard   5

How to Relieve the Frustration that
Comes as a Result of Wasting Huge
Portions of Your Life Trying to Solve
Computer Problems   11

If All This Should Fail   13

Secrets About Maintaining Privacy
in the Information Age   17

How To Computer-Train A Technotard
Who Has Zero Aptitude In High Tech   21

A Few More Ways You Can Cope with
Frustration and Anger Caused by
Computer Problems   27

There are Still a Few Pretty Cool
Things You Can Do In Life That Don't
Require a Gadget or a Screen   33

How to Get Free Help From
Tech People   37

A Few Things You Probably Shouldn't
Do When You are Really Worked Up
from Trying to Fix a Computer Problem   41

How to Avoid Having to Ever Interact
with Other Human Beings   43

1.1 When You are Determined to Remain Computer Illiterate Even if it Means you Will be Persecuted, Shunned, and Isolated.

Computers are evil. This is common knowledge. It is self-evident. I belong to a very secret group known surreptitiously as The League of International Computer Kwestioners and Yokels, or I.C.K.Y.. We are the only group I know of who is out there fighting to defend the rights of technotards. I mean, technotards are people, too and should have a few rights I would think.

There are millions of us! We at I.C.K.Y. think we need a bill of computer rights. For example, we think it would be cool if we had the right to be disconnected sometimes, the right to have a few moments each day when we are not frustrated, the right to keep our old phone for a few years if we're used to it, the right to be googled and have nothing harmful come up on the search, just for example.

Over the past few years, we technotards have watched these basic rights dwindle. And there is nothing worse than dwindling rights, unless you consider being eaten by sharks, having spiders take over your house, or spending all day trying to fix a computer glitch.

Dwindling rights are a recent phenomenon. Can you imagine if the British had had satellite G.P.S. to locate a fleeing Washington? Can you imagine Madison having to successfully maximize his search engines in order to convince New Yorkers to vote for the Bill of Rights? Can you imagine Lincoln posting the Gettysburg Address on his political blog instead of reading it live, or Jefferson tweeting out The Declaration of Independence? Or can you imagine Grant having Lee sign terms of surrender at the end of The Civil War electronically so he didn't have to hang around Appomatox, and then emailing it back to Washington D.C.?

No, Washington, Jefferson, Lincoln, and the Hessions didn't have to deal with political blogs, facebook, or G.P.S. They were technotards! They were highly successful despite having ZERO computer skills. So, that puts me and the rest of you technotards in pretty good company. I figure if Ben Franklin didn't have to figure out how to operate a computer, then neither should Justin Case.

Here are some danged good reasons to remain computer illiterate:

1. Your blood pressure will remain much lower.

2. If something accidentally falls out of your pocket into the toilet, it can't be your smart phone. You don't have one!

3. If you are a technotard and some burglar breaks into your house, he will have to look for something else to steal-that is something other than your electronics.

4. If you are going to get carpal tunnel syndrome, you will have to get it somewhere else other than from your computer.

5. If some thief wants to steal your money, he will have to do it the old fashioned way, by mugging you or breaking into your car, not by cyber-crime.

6. Instead of spending huge blocks of time trying to fix computer problems, you will remain free to use that time pulling weeds, trimming your mustache, doing laundry, training for a triathalon, or learning a new language.

7. If your children or grandchildren ask to play games on your mobile device, you can assume they want to borrow your horse to play polo or to use your tractor to play chicken, not to play angry birds, or fight imaginary aliens.

8. You won't have to struggle to stay ahead of the latest computer virus.

9. You can spend the money most people spend on high speed internet access on a new fishing motor, 8-track tapes, or a new metal detector.

10. You will never face the dilemma of whether or not to accept a friend request from someone you don't like.

There. Now, don't you feel better?

2.3 How to Know if You are a Technotard

Take our exclusive Technotard test:

Your favorite mobile device is a horse, pickup, or car.

◯ True   ◯ False

You still have a land line.

◯ True   ◯ False

You can no longer comprehend any advertising or billboards.

◯ True   ◯ False

The Joyful Techno-Tard

You are never chomping at the bit to get your hands on the latest gadget.
○ True   ○ False

You would rather have a colonoscopy or talk to an aggressive sales rep than go on line to buy something or to solve problems with your insurance.
○ True   ○ False

You don't know the brand name of the mobile device you are using, so you call it "Meg."
○ True   ○ False

You have no idea how the device you're using actually works.
○ True   ○ False

You don't comprehend the concept of "apps" or have any idea what an "app" actually is.
○ True   ○ False

You guard your device passionately, because every time you allow someone else to touch it, you can never make it work again like it did before.
○ True   ○ False

You hate it whenever new technology comes out because that means you will now have to work to re-learn some dumb routine tasks.
○ True   ○ False

You now have to plan to spend huge blocks of your time each day fiddling with your dumb machine trying to find out what's wrong so you can finish some simple task. It would be much easier to just call someone and pay them to solve the problem or do the task, but there is no one to call. Your only option is to interact with another machine.
○ True ○ False

You still prefer to read books made out of paper.
○ True ○ False

You pay your bills by check.
○ True ○ False

You really don't want the whole world to be privy to your sensitive private information.
○ True ○ False

You really don't want the whole world to know where you are every minute of every day and to follow you wherever you go electronically.
○ True ○ False

There are huge blocks of time each day when you actually turn off your devices to do other things. In fact, you actually enjoy being disconnected.
○ True ○ False

The Joyful Techno-Tard

You become irritated when people are using their device in your presence while you are teaching, lecturing, giving important instructions, or having a conversation face-to-face.

○ True ○ False

Some days you hate gadgets. Some days you loathe them. Some days you tolerate them. But every day you long for simpler times.

○ True ○ False

If you could do anything you want to the people who keep inventing new stuff and forcing it upon you, would it be:

○ A - Congratulate them and ask them all kinds of questions about future plans.

○ B - Ask them questions about applications you don't understand regarding your gadget.

○ C - You have no idea. You couldn't understand anything they say anyway.

○ D - Make really mean, but creative suggestions about what they can do with their latest gadget(s).

Essay 1: Describe your feelings whenever Apple releases its newest operating system or I-Pad.

Essay 2: Chronicle the history of the telephone in your life beginning with the party line and ending with the latest smart phone.

How To Score
Give yourself approximately one point for each true or false answer. Give yourself 20 points if you were smart enough to not bother taking the multiple choice part of the test. Grade your essays any way you want, the more whimsical the better. (That is how I grade my college students' essays.)

0-5 Points: You are comfortably tech savvy and may survive.

6-10 Points: There is a faint glimmer of technological hope for you. Sadly, for now your life stinks. I feel your pain. You are competent enough to keep trying to figure things out, not smart enough to ever get anything done without huge stress, but still not enough of a technotard to drop completely out of the game and just accept your worthlessness.

11-15 Points: With lots of help from your children and grandchildren, you may possibly be able to sometimes keep one nostril above water-technologically.

16-20 Points: You still haven't learned how to text.

21+ Points: You are a certified technotard, doomed to be cast aside on the rubbish heap of life, along with your super-8 movie camera, phonograph, and 8-track tapes.

3.2 How to Relieve the Frustration that Comes as a Result of Wasting Huge Portions of Your Life Trying to Solve Computer Problems

1. Pull all the hair off from your hamster, Sammie.

2. Yodel your version of Amazing Grace.

3. Give yourself a swirlie.

4. Give someone smaller than you a swirlie.

5. Over-eat; we recommend Bugles, jelly-filled donuts, Fritos, or potato salad.

6. Chop wood or break rocks with your fist. If that doesn't relieve your stress, try using your head.

7. Float face-down in the hot tub.

8. Float face-up in the hot tub.

9. Eat a gallon of chicken soup.

10. Peel the bark from all the trees in the neighborhood.

11. Drive really fast.

12. Drive really slow.

13. Alternate driving really fast and really slow.

14. Run a marathon.

15. Run two or more marathons.

16. Mow the lawn.

17. Pull out your nose hairs.

4.1 If All This Should Fail

If despite all you do, you are unable to get your technotard brain around electronics or fake your way into a high-paying job, here are a few non-traditional occupations you might have to try. I was a little reluctant to share these because I am naturally hopeful and optimistic, albeit incompetent. And some of these don't pay very well, but sometimes you just have to do what you just have to do. Let's face it, if you can't learn the computer, your options are pretty limited.

Here are a few alternative occupations for those who remain computer illiterate:

The Joyful Techno-Tard

1. Speed bump

2. Parachute tester

3. Professional blood donor (This is only for those who don't have hepatitis, and it assumes you haven't spent much time in foreign countries.)

4. Professional organ donor (Bear in mind, the downside of this career is that you have a finite number of kidneys.)

5. Bunji chord tester

6. Balloon or dirigible ballast

7. Land fill

8. Bullet proof vest tester

9. Coal mine timber

10. Crash test dummy

11. Park bench

12. Shooting target

13. Ski jump

14. Trampoline pad

15. Scenery holder

16. Mine-field safety checker

17. Retaining wall

18. Artillery shell

19. Crane balancing weight

20. Farm-field drag

Here is a comprehensive list of all careers, which no longer require extensive computer knowledge:

1. Septic pumping

5.7 Secrets About Maintaining Privacy in the Information Age

Every day millions of peoples' sensitive personal data is compromised as crooks, hackers, foreign governments, disoriented technotards, marketers, ex-spouses, and many others gather data on all of us, often with mal-intent.

Consider This:

G.P.S. can give anyone who wants to track you your precise location at all times-24/7.

Satellite images of your 5-year-old grandson watering the irises are on Google Earth for the whole world to see.

The stupid comments made when you were in a

drunken stupor and goofing off on Facebook will be available out in cyber-space for the rest of your life, and will form the basis of your personal historical record, handed down for generations.

Your delinquent bills and pathetic credit history are likely to come up on your ex-wife's computer screen and your IRS agent's smart phone when you thought you were deleting them.

A satellite image of the tattoo on your derriere, along with your derriere could easily wind up on your grandchild's computer 50-years from now when she is searching out her genealogy.

Now don't get all worked up. It's not all as bad as you are feeling. Actually, it's much worse. Your children who are fighting over your estate have access to all your medical records including extremely revealing x-rays of your enlarged prostate, and the news of your terminal hemor-rhoids.

At the moment when you are hurrying to down-load your credit card information to buy a football ticket, every company in America who wants to sell you something is given a detailed profile of your buying habits, including all your compulsive tendencies, weaknesses and vulnerabilities.

Lawyers working for the guy with whom you are competing for a promotion have the details of your 1988 nervous breakdown along with those of every site you were trapped in during the ten minutes when a pop-up porn promotion kept multiplying, making it impossible for you to get out of the site until you finally smashed your computer with a sledge.

Lawyers working for your ex-husband accessed your therapist's notes, including your frustrated rant about wanting him dead.

For the president's re-election campaign, his hacks have the information they need to blackmail you into voting for their candidate, and to seize all your bank accounts and your 401-K, in case they should run short on campaign funds and need to buy votes from someone else, or to improve his lifestyle.

So, what exactly can you do about it? Become a certified technotard, that's what. Instead of buying stuff on-line using your debit card, do your shopping at the farmers market using chickens for barter. Instead of applying for the job on-line, be unemployed and live off the land-dumpster diving. Instead of going on line to figure out why your account is overdrawn, ignore your overdraft and move in with your kids.

How to Maintain Privacy the Technotard Way:

1. Never get on a computer. They will bite you.

2. Avoid social media. Make friends and loved ones swear they will never

even mention your name on social media or any other electronic forum, and if anyone ever needs to refer to you, use a code name, such as Bozo, or Barbie.

3. Scrupulously avoid all electronic gadgets—including the toaster, microwave, and electric razor.

4. When you must communicate, do it with hand signals, carrier pigeon, or smoke signals.

5. Avoid any job requiring computer literacy. There are plenty of other jobs you can do such as septic pumping, pumping out septic tanks, or cesspool maintenance, just to name a few. (A complete list is included above.)

6. Don't ever use plastic to pay for anything. Pay for your airline tickets by barter, using shells, goats, or bushels of corn.

6.4 How To Computer Train A Techno-tard Who Has Zero Techno Aptitude

This problem is fundamentally the same as the problem of the parent who has to find a way to get his kid who has zero athletic ability onto the varsity baseball team, or the school counsellor who has to teach the girl with zero social skills how to get asked to Prom and then survive the date, or the parent whose child has zero academic skills to get him or her into a top-notch college. So, I asked myself, "How does a parent do this? It happens dozens of times every day somewhere in America." And I came up with a few simple answers.

First, take a close look at the kid who can't carry a tune in a bucket, whose parents are determined to get him onto the elite school choir despite his lack of aptitude and lack of interest. How do they do it? "Sympathy, that's how." Many hovering parents find a way to get those who are calling the shots to feel sorry for their kid. Some would go to the choir director with a concocted, sad tale of woe suggesting that the reason why this pathetic kid performed poorly in the audition is because they found him in an orphanage in southern Europe, where everyone knows people don't sing and treat their orphans poorly, if you don't count Prague or Budapest. If they can get the director to feel sorry enough for him, he just might put him in the choir out of sympathy.

Next, for the kid whose parents just have to get him or her into an elite academic institution, even if he would fail miserably when he gets there, the best way is fraud and deceit: In other words, these parents usually find a ringer to go take his entrance exams for him, hack into the school's computer system and fix his poor grades, take his math tests for him, and in all other ways, do some serious adult cheating on the kid's behalf. This strategy also sets the kid up for a lifetime of wonderful success in his career in the field of having his parents continue to fix things for him.

And finally, the parents who absolutely must have their daughter on the cheer leading squad or their son on the football team, even though she or he has zero talent, frequently rely on bribery. They might build the team a new practice facility, slip the coach a pile of money for new fancy uniforms, and contribute generously to the summer camp fund to make sure the coach gets paid in a manner to which she or he has become accustomed. This can be a very successful strategy, and will also help the student athlete make friends on the squad. Parents, all you have to do is give the kids on the squad lots of cool stuff if they promise to be your kid's buddy.

So, getting back to this problem of "helping" a person who has zero computer skills become functionally computer literate, since these skills are so indispensable now-a-days, we suggest you leave nothing to chance. If the person in question is a certified technotard, or if you are one and are struggling to survive in this high-tech world, we suggest you apply all three of these strategies at the same time. Fool people, bribe people, and make them feel sorry for you or for your kid.

Just to illustrate, in the case of computer literacy, this is how that strategy might look:

Part 1 – Fooling People:

Memorize a few words of computer-eze. Don't worry, you don't need to know too many of them, and you really don't need to know what they mean. Remember, you are going to fool people. Choose some words like, zip-drive, motherboard, twitter, binary, android, and pixels and begin to randomly insert them into your everyday language. In fact, you will really look smart if you combine some of these words into complex phrases. An example would be, "My, that's a snappy binary motherboard you're wearing!" or "I think I'll twitter on into town and grab some zip-drive androids."

Part 2 – Bribery:

In corporate America, the manager is the equivalent of the high school cheerleader or basketball coach. It will be he or she you will have to convince in order to get a high-paying job. So, before you waste a lot of money bribing ineffectively, do a little research to find out what this manager likes, what his or her weaknesses are, what bad things he has done, and if he is in debt-stuff like that. This information is readily available all over the internet. Just Google this person and see if you can find out what kinds of ads show up on his computer screen. Then, offer to buy everyone uniforms, pay for transportation, buy a cruise, cover his kids' college education, pay off a few gambling debts, etc.

Part 3 – Being Pathetic:

Just be prepared with a few embellished stories of how tough life is and then be sure to drag your foot behind you and drool.

Using all three strategies at once should make it impossible for him to turn you down. So this is how using all three strategies at once might look: Drool and drag your foot to the interview all the while talking about zip-drives, androids, and motherboards. And before you leave, be sure to stack a bit pile of $100.00 bills on his desk. You're in-guaranteed.

A Few More Ways You Can Cope with Frustration and Anger Caused by Computer Problems

1. Pull each hair out of your arms, one-at-a-time.

2. Pull the hair out of someone else's arms.

3. Lie down next to your pig and have a good wallow.

4. Go take a 48-hour nap.

5. Focus all your concentration on swallowing a few gold fish.

6. Drive your car off a cliff.

7. Use your computer mouse as a hockey puck.

8. Use your computer as a bowling ball.

9. Accidentally back over your device with a track hoe.

10. Accidentally back over it again.

11. Use your computer for target practice.

12. Go chop some wood.

13. See if you can do 100,000 pushups.

14. Stick your head under water and hold your breath for a long time.

15. Lock yourself inside your root cellar and yell until your voice is gone.

16. Crank up the stereo and sing the oldies as loud as you can.

17. Eat 20 chili dogs.

18. Throw up 20 chili dogs.

19. Kick the dog.

20. Kick your neighbor's dog.

21. Give a massage to someone you really don't like.

22. Pound your fists into a bag of marshmallows.

23. Bury your head in your pillow and scream.

24. Bunji Jump.

25. Walk on hot coals.

26. Eat 100 donuts.

27. Smash your guitar on your amplifier.

28. Run a 10-K backwards.

29. Wrestle a steer.

30. Go bull-riding.

31. Swim up-stream.

32. Do a series of belly flops off the high dive.

33. Go shear some sheep.

34. Climb a tall tree.

35. Climb a tall mountain.

36. Yodel as loud as you can.

37. Go jogging on all fours.

38. Make random crank phone calls and scream unintelligible nonsense into the phone. (Best to borrow someone else's phone to do this one.)

39. Hula dance for half-an-hour.

40. Start a good food fight.

8.9 There are Still a Few Pretty Cool Things You Can Do In Life That Don't Require a Gadget or a Screen

Unless you are a technotard, One of life's greatest trials can be having a day, or even a few minutes when you have to try to get along without your gadget or screen. Unfortunately, times come along in almost every life when a person has to survive without a device or gadget.

Exhibit A, B, C, and D: My sister dropped her device into the toilet, my brother-in-law dropped his device onto the concrete, my son's device just stopped working for some strange reason, my neighbor got herself into a tight spot and forgot to pay her wireless bill and so was disconnected for a time, my good friend had her purse stolen along with her device, my cousin's devices caught a virus, which ruined his motherboard, and so it goes. These are true-life situations, very much like a reality show, if you can think in those terms, and something like this could even happen to you. You should be prepared.

So, as part of your preparation, kind of like a savings account or food storage, here is a list of a few things you could do without a device or screen for a few minutes or for a couple of days if you have to. Some of them are even sort of worthwhile---at a certain level.

A few things you could do if you ever find yourself with a little time when you can't use your gadget:

1. Have a face-to-face conversation with another human being. (Some of us will need to practice with the dog for a couple of days first. It could cause trauma)

2. Go play catch with your kid. (This could cause your kid trauma. Use caution.)

3. Visit grandma or some other elderly technotard.

4. Get some physical exercise: walk, jog, ride a bike, hike, put weights on your arms when you push the keys. (Some will need to work up to things slowly or risk a stroke or heart attack.)

5. Fix things around the house you've been neglecting.

6. Build a treehouse with your son.

7. Build a dollhouse with your daughter.

8. Read a book...on paper. You can find these in many peoples' basements in a box. They're really quite common.

9. Bake cookies with your daughter.

10. Bake cookies with your mom.

11. Go fishing with your son.

12. Go fishing with yourself.

13. Go fishing with your dad.

14. Go rock-climbing.

15. Go mountain-biking.

16. Explore some beautiful place in nature...in person...in real time.

17. Visit someone who is lonely.

18. Visit someone whose spouse has died.

19. Help a neighbor put a roof on her house.

20. Go swimming.

9.5 How to Get Free Help From Tech People

Sadly there are no longer any companies, or for that matter individuals, who can get along without having their own tech specialist. Every week these days, a new piece of technology or app comes out, which we have to figure out or be left alongside the primrose path like some pile of rancid fish entrails. This is good news for computer people who are likely looking at full employment and exaggerated incomes in this seller's market for a long, long time. But for the rest of us, this is a nightmare.

Those suffering the worst are technotards. These times are an unmitigated disaster for us. Every week when that new device comes out, we are guaranteed weeks of frustration and high blood pressure as we try to figure it out. If anyone else ever picks up our device, we can be assured that they have done something to it and that it will never work right again. No matter how careful we are, even we ourselves, daily touch some spot on the screen, almost touch some key, or even wonder about touching something, which is all it takes to mess up our device so that a normal person can't figure out what he has done. We are up the crick.

If you are one who has to pay for tech help every time you find yourself with a new device or app, or every time someone messes with your gadget, you are facing certain financial ruin. So it is imperative that you master the skills of getting free help from techies. Fortunately, tech people aren't all that complicated and are generally pretty user-friendly. Here are a few suggestions.

A Few Suggestions

1. Have one of your daughters marry a tech person. (We did this and it works great.)

2. Keep in your kids and grandkids' good graces by buying them lots of cool stuff.

3. Tell your specified techie that you

are certain he can't fix your device
and that dozens of experts have tried
and failed.

4. Offer to pay him for helping you in
memory for his device, or in Doritos,
whichever he would prefer.

5. Frame your problem in dragon
language (Smuilian).

6. Convince him that hidden in the
solving of your problem is a Trojan
that can get him access to the
Pentagon's and C.I.A.'s master
computers.

7. Just be generally pathetic, playing
on his sympathies.

The Joyful Techno-Tard

10.1 A Few Things You Probably Shouldn't Do When You are Really Worked Up from Trying to Fix a Computer Problem

Trying to fix incomprehensible computer problems is a nightmare for technotards. It can leave us completely catatonic, trembling with frustration, or screaming in angst. Therefore, if you are a technotard, we recommend that you give it a little time after trying to solve exasperating computer problems before you try to do something else that is delicate, has life or death implications, involves emergency response vehicles, long-term contracts, marriage, divorce, travel to France, or is otherwise important or dangerous. This is a partial list of activities in which you should probably not participate immediately following a computer frustration episode.

Shortly After Unsuccessfully Trying to Solve a Computer Problem, Do Not:

1. Talk to your parole officer.

2. Visit with your IRS agent.

3. Handle eggs.

4. Teach a class on anger management.

5. Meet the tech support person you have been talking to, who doesn't speak English, and who lives in Nepal.

6. Drive on a narrow, mountain road.

7. Slug a window.

8. Pick a fight with a Navy Seal.

9. Try to fix your wristwatch.

10. Kick the steel bank vault door.

11.4 How to Avoid Having to Ever Interact with Other Human Beings

Let's face it. Other people can be a major pain in the backside. Virtually nobody feels exactly like you do about many, many things. They just don't understand.

Getting along with live people usually requires cooperation, compromise, and patience. Gratefully, developing these archaic virtues in this age of high-tech instant gratification, is completely unnecessary. Yes, if you struggle whenever interacting with real people, we are now at a stage when you can pretty much avoid them forever if you want to. You can do it by following these simple suggestions:

How to Avoid Contact With Other Human Beings

1. Live with your Mother in the basement room that has been yours since you were a kid. You can avoid ever having to interact with land lords, real-estate agents, and maintenance people. And as a bonus, you will never have to move your stuff-even that pile of dirty clothes. If Mom wants to talk to you, ask her to e-mail you. Of course, these e-mails can be ignored until you're ready to deal with her. She's not going to kick you out. She's your Mom.

2. Choose a career that allows you to work from home, such as computer game developer, or mattress tester. Apply for your jobs on-line. This way you will never have to leave the basement and risk running into someone who requires some human interaction.

3. Shop for everything you need on-line; even do your banking on-line. When the food and electronic gadgets you have bought arrive, your mom can get them from the U.P.S. guy and set them outside your door. Then, you can retrieve them when he coast is clear.

4. If, for whatever reason you are ever required to be out in public, simply ignore everyone and stay focused on your mobile device. Avoid making eye contact, which could cause someone to try to speak to you.

5. Keep your vocal chords from complete atrophy using a combination of the following:

Talking to yourself; Cussing people who don't know how to do things right; Using voice recognition sometimes to interact with your computer.

Some quotes by a few notable technotards

"I came up with the atom bomb and the theory of relativity all without a computer. In my day, our choices were a black board or a piece of paper."

~ Einstein

"Computer games?!? How about Olympic games?"

~ Jim Thorpe

"Despite being severely technotarded, I still managed to write some pretty cool music."

~ Motzart

"We didn't need some stupid computer to build the pyramids."

~ Ramses II

"I conquered most of Europe without a cell phone or other mobile device."
~ Napoleon Bonaparte

"Just think, all that time I thought I was stupid, and I just had a different type of intelligence."
~ King Solomon

"Try ruling the world without so much as a flip phone."
~ Queen Elizabeth I

"When I made myself Emperor of Rome, I had never even heard of a computer."
~ Julius Caesar

"I'm afraid a cell phone would just have been a distraction as we fought the British. Besides, who would I have texted? The cell phone services were unbelievably slow."
~ Joan of Arc

"So what exactly do you think I would have done with a mobile device? Email my thesis onto the door of the Cathedral at Worms?
~ Martin Luther

"None of the animals had phones and the ark didn't have a wireless network, so I really can't see how things would have been any better. On second thought, the Weather Channel would have been a really nice thing to have."

~ Noah

"...still trying to phone home. Can you hear me now?"

~ E.T.

12.6

The Advantages of Texting

As I'm sure you know, I do not usually crow about the benefits of technology. Normally, I despise technology. However, there is one relatively new technology that we may want to consider: texting. Texting is an example of one technology that has a few benefits-possibly even enough for you technologically challenged to want to learn how. To help us technotards try to make an intelligent decision about whether or not to try to learn how to text, I provide these examples of some of the advantages to texting.

Some Advantages to Texting

1. We all know people who can't shut up. We hate to go see them or even to talk to them on the phone because we know that every time we do,

they will end up wasting huge chunks of our time droning on and on about politics or complaining about hemorrhoids or something. Who hasn't been trapped listening to someone ramble on and on while he is left doing everything he can think of to signal to this person he is finished with the conversation. He nods off to sleep. He acts bored. He becomes distracted. He does all these things and more, but to no avail. This person talks on and on and on while he misses his wedding, appointment with his parole officer, or his bypass surgery. So we all spend important portions of our lives trying to avoid people like this.

What's cool about texting is it gives you an alternative. When you text a person who is hard to get away from, all he or she can do is text you back...or ignore you. If he or she calls, you know who it is with caller I.D., and you don't have to answer if you don't want to. So, if this obnoxious person is important in your life, you can still communicate by text message. And you can do it and remain in complete control. (Hint: the more difficult or irritating you are, the more text messages you will get relative to phone calls.)

2. While you are texting, no one can see the expression on your face. You can be raging in anger, rolling on the floor laughing, or exploding in incredulity, and the person you are texting will assume you are calm as a cucumber...unless you send a bunch of lol's and smiley faces as part of your text message.

3. Texting is another cool way to interrupt or end a conversation when you need to. Because you are using a gadget to communicate, you can pause any time you want to, for hours or days if need be, and then pick up your gadget and continue the conversation days or even months later. They will have no idea why you stopped texting unless you tell them. For all they know, you are dead.

4. When you need to send a message that someone is irrelevant or unimportant, one of the easiest ways I know is simply by texting in the middle of a conversation. We have all been talking to someone who has been interrupted by a cell message, which apparently required an immediate response. I don't know about you, but when this has happened to me, I certainly got the message of how important I was compared to the person texting.

5. Texting while driving can be another means of multitasking enabling us all to get more done and to make other drivers extremely angry, and occasionally even get our insurance to buy us a new car.

So there you have it, technotards, in certain cases, texting may be one technology you could consider.

13.7 Apps We Would Like to See

1.   The tie-into-your-brain app. This is the ultimate in hands-free technology. You think it and your device instantly responds. (Some of you sociopaths and sick-o's may want to consider passing on this app.)

2.   The pay-day app. It causes your device to manufacture money from cyberspace. (Also known as the modern-day politician's app.)

3.   The bureaucracy app-translates

jargon and acronyms into old fashioned
English.

4.   The diner bell app-cranks out
burgers and fries.

5.   The honey-do app-washes the
dishes, cleans the house, and fixes
dinner.

6.   The dragon's voice app-makes
obnoxious people go away.

7.   The detail app-cleans inside
your car.

8.   The ultimate medical app-cures
your cold and flu.

9.   The farmer Brown app-milks the
cow and gathers the eggs.

10.   The headache preventing app-
makes all your decisions for you.

11.   The alternative medicine app-goes
to your doctor's appointments for you.

12. The supermodel app—makes you better looking.

13. The Zumba app—does your exercise for you.

14. You should think of a few apps you would like to see. About all we have to do to get the app is bet a few tech guys they can't do it. A few years later some entrepreneurial dot com will be selling it.

14.9

Trouble shooting for Techno-tards: How to fix what's wrong with your gadget

One of the reasons why we technotards so despise technology is that whenever there is a problem, we are up the proverbial crik without a paddle. There is no way we can ever fix anything. So we are left seething in frustration.

But then again, maybe this doesn't have to be. I am a confirmed technotard, who have thought extensively about this problem and I have come up with some great strategies for fixing your stuff that you can do all by yourself, maybe even without the help of your grandkids. Really! Try these strategies. They just might change your life.

Symptom:

Random parts from your device are dribbling onto the floor behind you as you walk to the car.

Likely Problem:

When you let your three-year-old daughter use your gadget to look at pictures, she got frustrated when she was unable to find the one with the puppy, so she threw your device onto the floor and sat on it, exposing an obvious design flaw.

Solution:

First, obtain a small screwdriver. Next, begin to gather up what parts you can find so you can use most of them later. (Be sure and look in your daughter's mouth for the ones she found.) Then, place these parts into the bottom of your flower pot, add soil and Miracle Grow fertilizer or a little compost, and plant a geranium. When you finish, go buy another gadget. Yours is toast.

Symptom:

Water, Mountain Dew, or coffee is oozing out of cracks in your device.

Likely Problem:

When you dropped your device into the toilet, spilled your pop on it, or inadvertently left it in your pocket when you were nominated to be on the dunk-tank at the fair, the fluid seeped inside. (Sadly, this problem exposes a common design flaw-a lack of water resistance common in many gadgets, which consumer advocates have failed to convince the industry to fix.)

Solution:

Remove battery, place battery and gadget in bowl filled with dry rice or some other grain. Add chicken bouillon, chunks of pre-cooked chicken breast meat, vegetables, salt, and bring to a boil. Simmer for 30 minutes over medium heat, and serve with garnish of your choice. Then borrow someone else's gadget to get along until you have time to go buy a new one. Your gadget is fried.

Symptom:

The screen on your device has a crack...or multiple cracks.

Most Likely Problem:

When you put your gadget into your back pocket and sat down on the bleachers, you most likely bent it into a "V" exposing an obvious design flaw. Then, when you tried to straighten it back out you failed to heat the device to 1200 degrees, and since the metal and glass were not pliable at room temperature, the screen broke, exposing another obvious design flaw.

Solution:

Carefully remove broken glass using a razor blade. Then, using super glue or gorilla glue, piece the screen back together. Next, place the device flat onto your dining room table where your friends can use it as a coaster, because its days as an electronic gadget are over. If you intend to continue telecommunicating with your friends and neighbors, you may need to get yourself a new gadget.

Symptom:

Your gadget is operating very slowly. It took two weeks to open an e-mail from your daughter telling you that she has been abducted and held for ransom, and in which she is begging for you to pay the ransom within 48 hours.

Most Likely Problem:

You have picked up the latest super virus named Stanley, along with 4 Trojans, and a few-dozen random spy-ware plants. You also have 10,000 un-deleted text-messages with u-tube video attachments and another 7500 undeleted e-mails, and the personal information you have been leaving all over the internet in the wake of expensive credit-card purchases suggests that you are rich enough that the Russian Mafia believes it can make a fortune kidnapping your daughter.

Solution:

Start by deleting at least 5000 of your messages and e-mails. Next, try to back up your important data onto a paper notebook or tin-can since the motherboard on your device is fried, which exposes an obvious design flaw. Then, find a calm lake and skip your device across the surface, because you might as well get some small enjoyment from it, since you will be buying a new one. Work on getting your daughter back so she can help you set up your new device with better firewalls and other protection for your device. And consider concealed weapons training for non-expendable family members, or at least a can of pepper spray.

Symptom:

You are going crazy listening to the same ring tone play over and over and over and over.

Most Likely Problem:

The person who set up your ring tone is an idiot.

Solution:

Find a 14-year-old kid who is willing to help you. Then, choose a song you already hate. Have said 14-year-old help you make this hated song your ring tone and have it play at chipmunk speed, thereby shortening the length of time you have to listen to it and saving songs that you don't already hate so you can enjoy them later.

Symptom:

When you tap the screen on your device, rubber chickens and weasels pop out.

Most Likely Problem:

Your gadget had weasels and rubber chickens in it. Some prankster you know is probably trying to be funny.

Solution:

This exposes an obvious design flaw that can only be corrected by buying another gadget. Thankfully, during the time you have been reading this chapter, your current gadget has become obsolete and so, if you didn't need to buy one because of the weasels and chickens, you must buy one because your old software and apps are no longer compatible with the work you need to do on your gadget.

More Apricot Press Humor Books

"In a world where some people may not want any part of your attitude, the sharing skills taught in this book are a must have."

Paperback $7.95 U.S.

"Maybe you're just sick and tired of being wealthy and you're ready to try something else for a change, like poverty. Whatever your circumstances, we know this book is for you."

Paperback $7.95 U.S.

"Instructions for becoming the Geezer you have always dreamed of. Geezing is not as easy as it looks. It's definitely not for sissies."

Paperback $7.95 U.S.

"This book is for the few who are silently bearing the burden of a superior intelligence, or think they are anyway..."

Paperback $7.95 U.S.

"OK, so you're having a bad day, maybe a whole slew of them in rapid succession. You've tried whining, you've tried complaining and nobody cares."

Paperback $7.95 U.S.

"If we are to understand the urge in man to fish, we must dig down through the strata of dirt and rocks and compost deep into the earth, back to primitive man to find our clues..."

Paperback $7.95 U.S.

"People today are worried. We worry that the economy will go into the tank, causing us to get laid off from our job as quality control tester at the dental floss foundry..."

Paperback $7.95 U.S.

"If you have seen more than a few sunsets, you may be starting to suspect that life is not fair. This book provides more evidence."

Paperback $7.95 U.S.

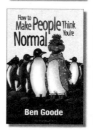

"If this book is in your hip pocket when a dog bites you, it could save your tattoo. It contains humor for people who are so smart, normal people don't understand them..."

Paperback $7.95 U.S.

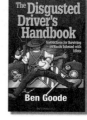

"A must read for anyone trying to stay sane while driving on today's idiot infested roads."

Paperback $7.95 U.S.

Order Online! www.apricotpress.com

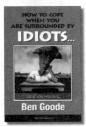
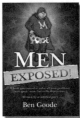
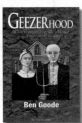

Enjoy our on-line magazine at:
thesleepyriverjournal.com

Apricot Press Order Form

Book Title	Quantity	x Cost / Book	= Total

All humor books are $7.95 US.

Do not send Cash. Mail check or money order to:
**Apricot Press   P.O. Box 98
Nephi, Utah   84648**
Telephone 435-623-1929
Allow 3 weeks for delivery.

Quantity discounts available.
Call us for more information.
9 a.m. - 5 p.m. MST

Sub Total =

Shipping = $2.00

Tax 8.5% =

Total Amount
Enclosed =

Shipping Address

Name:

Street:

City: State:

Zip Code:

Telephone: 63

Email: